Cats

CHELSEA CLUBHOUSE
An Imprint of Chelsea House Publishers
A Haights Cross Communications Company
Philadelphia

June Loves

Chelsea Clubhouse
1974 Sproul Road, Suite 400
Broomall, PA 19008-0914

The Chelsea House world wide web address is www.chelseahouse.com

Library of Congress Cataloging-in-Publication Data

Loves, June.
  Cats / June Loves.
  v. cm. — (Pets)

  Contents: Cats — Kinds of cats — Parts of a cat — Kittens — Choosing pet cats — Caring for pet cats — Feeding — Grooming — Training — Visiting the vet — Cat shows — Feral cats.

  ISBN 0-7910-7548-6
  1. Cats—Juvenile literature. [1. Cats. 2. Pets.] I. Title.
  SF445.7 .L68 2004
  636.8—dc21

                            2002155666

First published in 2003 by
MACMILLAN EDUCATION AUSTRALIA PTY LTD
627 Chapel Street, South Yarra, Australia, 3141

Associated companies and representatives throughout the world.

Page layout by Domenic Lauricella
Photo research by Legend Images

Printed in China

Acknowledgements
The author and the publisher are grateful to the following for permission to reproduce copyright material:

Cover photograph: girl with pet cat, courtesy of Getty Images.

ANT Photo Library, pp. 22, 30; Jean-Paul Ferrero/Auscape, pp. 6, 12 (top); Jean-Michel Labat/ Auscape, p. 7; Yves Lanceau/Auscape, pp. 18, 26; John McCammon/Auscape, p. 19; Getty Images, pp. 1, 4; Pelusey Photography, pp. 8–9, 12 (bottom), 13, 14, 16–17, 20, 21, 24, 25, 27, 28, 29; Photography Ebiz, pp. 5, 10; Sarah Saunders, pp. 15, 23; Michael Wintrip, p. 11.

While every care has been taken to trace and acknowledge copyright, the publisher tenders their apologies for any accidental infringement where copyright has proved untraceable. Where the attempt has been unsuccessful, the publisher welcomes information that would redress the situation.

Contents

Cats

Cats are popular pets. They are small enough to live indoors. Cats can be friendly and playful pets.

Some cats like to be held.

Some cats like to lie in the grass.

Some cats spend time outdoors. Owners may use a **lead**, or leash, to take their cats outside for exercise. Pet cats need food, water, **grooming**, and loving care every day.

Kinds of Cats

There are many kinds of pet cats. They can be divided into short-haired or long-haired groups. Different **breeds** belong to each group.

Short-haired cats

- ✪ Burmese
- ✪ Siamese
- ✪ Russian blue

Long-haired cats

- ✪ Persian
- ✪ Turkish Angora

This cat belongs to the short-haired group.

Pedigree cats are bred to have particular features.

Siamese cats have pale fur on their bodies and darker fur on their ears, **muzzle**, tail, and paws.

Parts of a Cat

A cat is a **mammal**. Some cats have slender bodies. Other cats have thicker bodies.

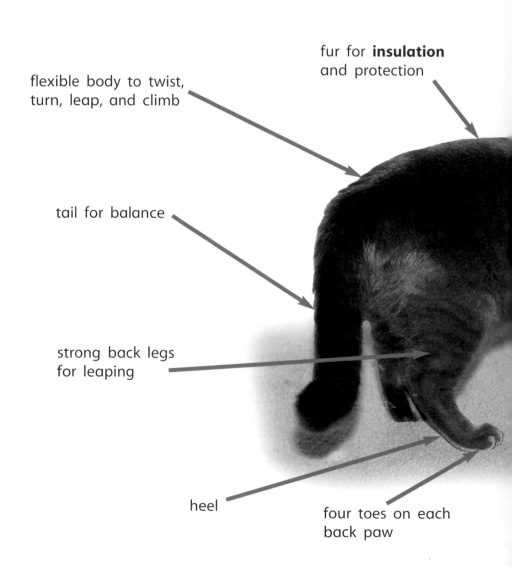

fur for **insulation** and protection

flexible body to twist, turn, leap, and climb

tail for balance

strong back legs for leaping

heel

four toes on each back paw

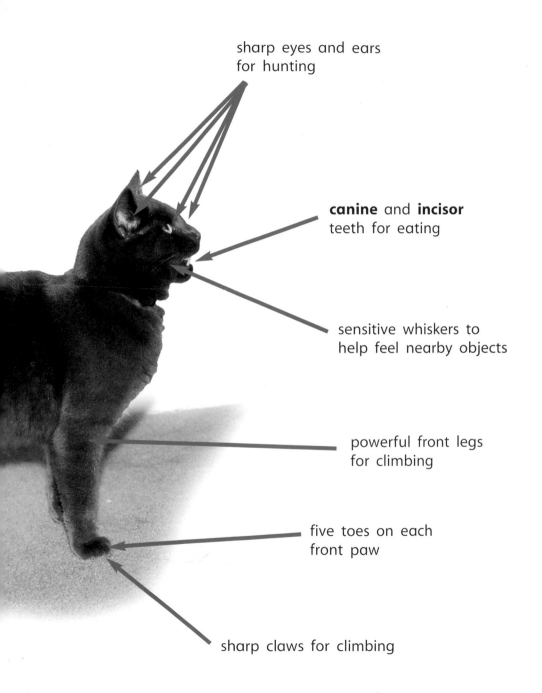

sharp eyes and ears
for hunting

canine and **incisor**
teeth for eating

sensitive whiskers to
help feel nearby objects

powerful front legs
for climbing

five toes on each
front paw

sharp claws for climbing

Fur

Cats have two layers of fur. The layer next to their skin is short and soft. The top layer is longer and stiffer.

Calico cats have patches of black, orange, and cream.

Whiskers

Whiskers help a cat sense the size and shape of nearby objects. At night, a cat uses its whiskers to feel for things that could get in its way.

Whiskers help a cat know whether it can fit through a small space.

Kittens

Mother cats usually have about four kittens in a **litter**. When kittens are born, their eyes are shut. They are helpless and need their mother's milk for eight weeks.

The mother cat chooses a safe place to have her litter.

Kittens' eyes start to open at seven to ten days.

12

Kittens are cats that are younger than nine months old.

Kittens start to walk after three weeks.

At four weeks of age, kittens discover how to play with one another. They also learn how to wash themselves.

Choosing Pet Cats

Choose cats or kittens with shiny, clean fur and bright eyes. Friendly, active kittens make good pets.

Pet stores sometimes have cats or kittens for adoption.

Animal shelters have many cats and kittens that need homes.

You can choose a kitten when it is about eight weeks old. You can adopt homeless kittens or cats from an animal shelter.

Caring for Pet Cats

Prepare a bed and **litter box** before you bring pets home. These are some supplies you may want to care for your cat.

scratching post

bedding

brush and comb for grooming

toys

a warm bed that is easy to clean

bowls for food and water

collar with an identification tag and bell

Place the litter box in a quiet place away from your cat's food. You will need to scoop waste out of the litter box every day.

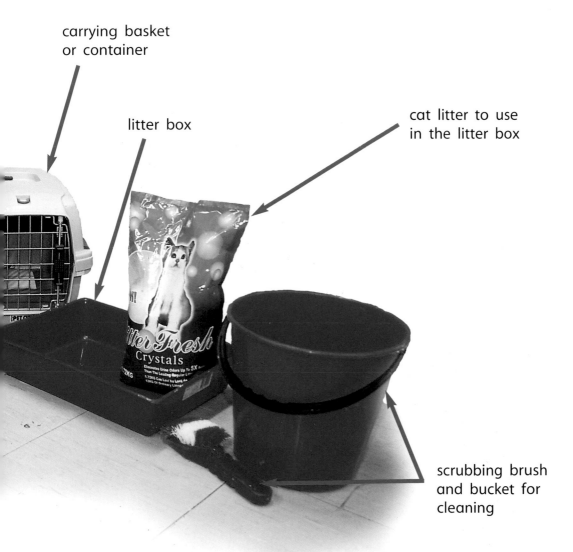

carrying basket or container

litter box

cat litter to use in the litter box

scrubbing brush and bucket for cleaning

Play time

Cats play to keep fit. When kittens tumble and play together, they are learning to get along with one another. You can have fun if you join in and play with your cat.

Cats like to chase and bat at toys.

Sleep time

Cats spend about two-thirds of their lives taking cat naps or sleeping. When cats take a cat nap, they sometimes curl up.

Cats sometimes have a floppy, uncurled body when they are in a deep sleep.

Feeding

Cats need to be fed every day. You can buy dry or canned food from a pet store or supermarket. Kittens should eat kitten food during their first year.

There are many kinds of food for cats and kittens.

Cats need fresh water every day.

Wash the food and water bowls every day.
Make sure your cat always has clean water.

Hunting for food

In the wild cats hunt for their food. If pet cats are allowed to run free outside, they may hunt mice, birds, and other small animals.

Cats may hunt mice or other small animals.

Cats can see well at night.

Cats are night hunters. At night, the **pupils** in their eyes open to catch as much light as possible. During the day, the pupils are narrow slits.

Grooming

Long-haired cats need brushing every day to stop tangles in their fur. Short-haired cats only need brushing once or twice a week to remove old hairs. You can check your cat for **fleas** at grooming time.

Brushing makes your cat's coat shiny and healthy.

Cats wash themselves very well. A cat's tongue is very rough and acts like a comb when it licks its fur. Cats bathe themselves several times a day.

Cats lick their front paws to wash their heads.

Training

House-train your cat to use the litter box to wet and leave its droppings. You can also train your cat to sharpen its claws on a scratching post, instead of the furniture.

Some scratching posts are made of wood. Others are wrapped in carpet or rope.

Using a lead is a safe way to take pet cats outside.

Some cats can be trained to walk on a lead. The lead needs to be hooked to a harness so it does not slip.

Visiting the Vet

Even if your cat seems healthy, it needs to visit the **vet** once a year. The vet will give your cat **vaccinations** and a check-up. Your vet may talk to you about **neutering**. Neutering keeps cats from having young.

Regular visits to the vet will keep your cat healthy.

Cat Shows

Sometimes owners enter their pet cats in shows. Owners groom their cats so their pets look the best. Cats are judged and winners are awarded prizes.

Judges look for cats with good features.

Feral Cats

Feral cats are cats that have gone wild. They kill many **native** animals and may carry diseases that could infect pet cats.

Feral cats hunt for their food.

Glossary

breeds	animals that belong to the same scientific group and have a similar appearance
canine	a long, sharp tooth near the front of the mouth
fleas	tiny insects that live in the fur of some animals; flea bites cause an animal's skin to itch
grooming	brushing or combing a pet to keep it clean
incisor	a short front tooth
insulation	a way of keeping heat and cold in or out
lead	a long rope that hooks onto an animal's collar or harness; also called a leash
litter	animals born at the same time to the same mother; also, a sand-like material used in a litter box to absorb a cat's waste and droppings
litter box	a tray where pets can wet and leave their droppings
mammal	a warm-blooded animal covered with hair whose young feed on their mother's milk
muzzle	an animal's nose and mouth
native	an animal or plant that lives in a certain area
neutering	an operation that prevents an animal from having young
pedigree	a pure-bred cat whose birth has been registered with an official cat club
pupils	the black parts of an animal's eyes; a pupil controls how much light enters the eye
vaccinations	medicine injected into people or animals to protect them from diseases
vet	a doctor who treats animals; short for veterinarian

Index